contents

introduction

PRESS FOR ACTION is designed to meet the needs of teachers anxious to use stimulating material with their students. Each double page spread provides a range of activities which encourage and promote student participation.

Each unit is well illustrated and the format throughout the book has been carefully thought out to make the material as user-friendly as possible. All material has been extensively trialed in the classroom.

1066-1500 is intended for pupils at Key Stage 3 and provides quality teaching materials which address many of the skills and concepts of National Curriculum. The activities are based upon topics taken from Core Study Unit 2 (KS 3) of National Curriculum, i.e. Medieval Realms: Britain 1066-1500.

1066-1500 is a collection of photocopiable resource sheets which can be used to provide a series of self-contained 'lessons' but it is also a flexible learning package for National Curriculum students of the 1990s.

Teaching Notes

With a few exceptions, all activities within the book can be attempted using the material and information provided. However, access to a Resource Centre/Library will enable students to develop some of the activities and go beyond the **One Step further.....** activities.

using PFA

BRIEF SYNOPSIS OF UNIT CONTENT

UNIT TITLE GIVING A BROAD INDICATION OF CONTENT

courts and punishments.....1

There was no prison system in the Middle Ages and crimes were punished in different ways.....

Some crimes were obvious, such as murder, robbery or assault. A serious crime was tried at a county court by a judge. Twelve men had to give evidence about the crime and the character of the person accused, and then the judge decided if the accused was guilty or not.

To help to keep law and order men over twelve were sometimes part of a TYTHING system. Groups of ten men had to keep an eye on each other, and their leader had to report on any misbehaviour to the county sheriff at a special court held every six months. This system got too difficult to administer, and gradually died out by about 1400.

VARIETY OF VISUAL STIMULI

Law and order was kept by villagers or townspeople themselves. In small communities it was difficult to commit a crime and get away with it. When the lord or baron (or his steward) visited the village he would listen to the wrongdoings and decide on punishments.

A CONSTABLE was chosen by a village to keep order during daylight. Towns would sometimes employ a constable, but most had to do their own work as well. It was an unpopular and thankless job, so most constables did it very badly in the hope that they wouldn't have to do it again.

HUE AND CRY simply meant that anyone who saw a crime being committed had a duty to shout it out and chase the criminal. If they didn't do this, the witness could also be punished. This was a very effective way of stopping crime, if it was witnessed.

At night in towns there was a CURFEW. This meant a bell was rung, and all honest people were meant to stay indoors. Sometimes a group of men would patrol the streets, they were called the WATCH. All men had to take their turn in the watch, but because this meant losing a night's sleep the watch didn't do a very good job. There were no street lights, so it was easy for criminals to escape.

- What do you think was the most effective way of keeping law and order in medieval times?
- Why was it very difficult to prove who had committed a crime?
- Whose final responsibility was law and order?
- Why was a person's reputation and character so important?

One step further .....

- For each method of keeping law and order, make a list of the good and bad points.
- Make up a dramatic scene in which a criminal is caught using one of these methods.

© 1992 Folens Limited   This page may be photocopied for classroom use only   1

courts and punishments.....2

There was no prison system in the Middle Ages. The most serious crimes were punished by death, and people accused of serious crimes were kept in the dungeons of the nearest lord until their trial.

The most common punishment was a fine of money or goods. This was paid to the person who was wronged, or to the court.

Other punishments relied on humiliation. Drunks would be put in the pillory or stocks, where people could laugh at them. Someone who sold bad goods would be dragged round the town on a hurdle (gate), with the bad goods displayed. A baker might be forced to eat his mouldy bread, a wineseller might have to drink his bad wine.

People who offended against the church laws had to perform a public penance. They might have to walk barefoot, or even on their knees, to church. Perhaps they would have to confess their wrongdoing to the whole congregation in church.

Women could be ducked in a pond, or were made to wear a special bridle to hold their tongue still, if they were accused of trying to boss their husband. They might have their hair shaved off if they got too concerned for their appearance.

Criminals could also be mutilated. They might be beaten or flogged, this was a punishment for persistent beggars. They might have their cheek or hand branded with the initial of their crime, or a hole bored through their ear. Ears, noses, hands and feet might be chopped off.

These punishments seem unfair, sexist and harsh. But English justice was famous all over the world, because there was no punishment without trial.

- Why were there no prisons in the Middle Ages?
- Fines were very commonly used as a punishment. Why was this a good idea?
- What was the point of humiliating a criminal? Why was this a good idea?
- What was the point of mutilation? How might this stop crime?

One step further .....

- Hangings and beheadings were public entertainment in medieval times. Why do you think the public were encouraged to take an active role in punishing criminals?
- Do you agree with punishments like mutilation and hanging? You might like to organise a class debate on the reasons for this type of punishment, and whether it works.
- English justice was famous all over the world. What does this tell you about the systems of justice in other countries?

© 1992 Folens Limited   This page may be photocopied for classroom use only   Page 19

RANGE OF ACTIVITIES TO STIMULATE AND EXTEND ALL ABILITIES

A WIDE RANGE OF SOURCES-BOTH WRITTEN AND VISUAL

EXTENSION WORK

Each unit in this book provides learning material for a range of ability levels and students should be encouraged to work at their own pace. Additionally, the resources are designed to provide a stimulus for both group and class discussion.

attainment target matrix

The numbers on the matrix refer to pages where the questions are suitable for the Attainment Target/ Level.

Questions appropriate to levels 1 and 2 are included to accommodate less able pupils in mixed ability classes. It is anticipated however, that teacher support will be given to assist these pupils with the source material.

It is hoped that teachers will discuss the worksheets in order to provoke a higher level of response.

	A.T.1a Change and Continuity	A.T.1b Causes and Consequences	A.T.1c Knowledge and Understanding	A.T.2 Interpretation	A.T.3 Using Sources
Level 1	10, 47			32	15, 17
Level 2	12, 14, 47	9, 23, 24, 27, 28	21, 26, 28	33	15, 17, 23, 31
Level 3	12, 14, 20, 22, 37, 40, 42, 43, 47	9, 20, 23, 24, 34, 35, 37, 38, 45	8, 29, 34, 37, 42, 43, 44	9, 17, 28, 29	10, 11, 15, 17, 26, 31, 33, 37, 39
Level 4	14, 16, 20, 31, 42, 43, 47	9, 17, 19, 22, 25, 34, 35, 38, 39, 40, 41, 42, 43	16, 24, 25, 26, 28, 29, 33, 42, 43	17, 38, 39	13, 15, 31
Level 5	32, 42, 43	22, 30, 34, 35, 36, 38, 39, 40	12, 18, 19, 23, 31, 33, 42, 43, 46	29, 32	15, 38
Level 6	29, 30, 32, 38, 47	32, 34, 35, 36, 38, 39, 41, 42, 43	25, 27, 28, 30, 32, 33, 42, 43, 44, 46	33, 34, 35, 38	15, 18
Level 7	21, 40, 42, 43, 44, 47	34, 35, 38, 40, 42, 43	27, 28	17, 29, 33	15, 38

timeline

1000	
	Edward the Confessor
1100	
1200	
1300	
1400	
1500	

1044 - 1066	Edward the Confessor
1066	Harold II
1066 - 1087	William I
1087 - 1100	William II
1100 - 1135	Henry I
1135 - 1154	Stephen
1154 - 1189	Henry II
1189 - 1199	Richard I
1199 - 1216	John
1216 - 1272	Henry III
1272 - 1307	Edward I
1307 - 1327	Edward II
1327 - 1377	Edward III
1377 - 1399	Richard II
1399 - 1413	Henry IV
1413 - 1422	Henry V
1422 - 1461	Henry VI
1461 - 1483	Edward IV
1483	Edward V
1483 - 1485	Richard III
1485 - 1509	Henry VII

● Mark the dates shown on the timeline and label the reign of each king. The first one has been done for you.

NOTE: 1mm = 2 years

1066: the background.....1

The Norman Conquest.....

Saxon England was governed in 'shires'. Many of these still exist today as counties. Each shire would be looked after on behalf of the king by an EAORL, appointed by the king. The Eaorl collected taxes for the governing of the country, and was in charge of the FYRD, or army, for his area.

The Eaorls and other wise men helped the king to rule the kingdom, and met together in Winchester to give him advice. This meeting was called the WITAN. The Witan and king had the job of choosing the next king to rule the country. It was most important that the king should be a good warrior, able to beat off invaders. The Saxon kingdom was under almost constant attack for about 650 years.

- Which groups attacked England?
- Why did Saxon Kings choose Eaorls who were good warriors?
- What effect would constant attacks from abroad have on daily life?

One step further .....

- If you were a member of the Witan, decide what type of king you would choose.
- The Saxons were fond of stories about warriors. Make up or illustrate your own story.

1066: the background.....2

When King Edward I died in 1066, there were three men who thought they had the right to the throne.

Harold Godwinsson	Harald Hardrada	William of Normandy
English	*Viking (Norwegian)*	*Norman (French)*

Chosen by Edward on his deathbed. A strong warrior. Had fought Edward's wars for him when he was old. Edward's choice, approved by the Witan.	Harold's brother Tostig supported him. A strong warrior. England's kings had been Vikings from 1016 to 1042.	Claimed Edward promised him the throne in 1051. Harold Godwinsson had promised to make William king, while he was William's hostage in 1064.

NAME	SHOULD BE KING	SHOULD NOT BE KING

- Complete the table. Put the good reasons for each man becoming king in one column, and the reasons for him not becoming king in the other.
- Use the results of your table to decide who had the best right to the throne.

One step further .....

- Organise your class into three groups. Each group should argue on behalf of one of the men. Imagine you are the Witan and have to decide who should be king.
- What was the likely outcome of this argument, whoever became king?

the battles of 1066.....1

The Normans and Saxons had different styles of fighting and different weapons. This difference may help to explain why the Normans won the Battle of Hastings.....

WILLIAM
⇦ □ □ □ □

HAROLD
⬅ ▬ ▬ ▬ ▬

BATTLE OF STAMFORD BRIDGE
25th Sept

YORK

HARALD HARDRADA BEATS THE YORKSHIRE FYRD
20th Sept

HULL

18th Sept
HARALD HARDRADA LANDS

1st Oct
HAROLD HEARS OF WILLIAMS INVASION

190 miles

WILLIAM IS CROWNED
25th Dec

WALLINGFORD

LONDON

5th Jan
Edward dies

HAROLD DECIDES TO FIGHT
13th Oct

60 miles

14th Oct
BATTLE OF HASTINGS

29th Sept
WILLIAM LANDS

HASTINGS

PEVENSEY

28th Sept
WILLIAM LEAVES NORMANDY

ST VALERY

NORMANDY

BAYEUX

NOTE
Battle of Stamford Bridge: On 25th September the Vikings, led by Harald Hardrada, were completely defeated by Harold's army.

➡

- Draw a timeline for the events of 1066.
- How well prepared was Harold to face invasion?

One step further .....

- The average marching pace is about three miles an hour. How long should it have taken Harold to march from:
    London to York?
    York to Hastings?

the battles of 1066.....2

ENGLISH

NORMAN

- Complete the table showing the different sorts of weapons, armour and equipment used by each side.
- What type of fighting was used by each side?

	ENGLISH	NORMAN
Weapons		
Armour		
Equipment		

One step further .....

- The horseback fighting used by the Normans gave them several advantages. Work out what these are, and then draw a picture of a Norman horseman attacking a Saxon warrior and using these techniques.
- Why did the Normans win the Battle of Hastings? Make a list of as many of the reasons as you can.

the importance of king.....1

When Duke William of Normandy conquered England in 1066, he introduced new ideas of kingship into England. The king had always been important, but now he owned all of the land and people of England, as he had beaten them in battle.....

Although the king owned everything in England, he could not possibly administer all of the lands himself. So he gave about half of the land to his supporters to look after for him. They were known as TENANTS-IN-CHIEF. In return for their land, they swore an oath of FEALTY. This was a promise to serve and obey the king. They also had to collect his taxes and raise soldiers for his armies. If a tenant-in-chief broke his oath, he lost his land. But as a tenant they could claim protection and justice from the king.

The church also gained by the conquest of England. William I gave about a quarter of his land to the church. The bishops administered the land for the king as tenants-in-chief.

The tenants-in-chief could not look after the lands they had been given, as these were often scattered all over the country. So they further divided the land among their followers, who also had to swear an oath of fealty in return. These men were knights who had fought with them, or other gentlemen.

Very few of the ordinary people of England actually owned any property. They were owned by the knight or baron who held their land, and in return for their land they had to work for a certain number of days on their lord's land, or to serve as a soldier for him in times of war. The lord had a duty to administer justice and protection to villagers on his land.

- Imagine you are a knight who fought for William. Write down what you have gained through the Conquest.
- As a knight, what do you owe your lord? What does he owe you in return?
- As a knight, who owes you duties? What do you owe in return?

One step further .....

- Find out the different types of ownership of property that exist today. Which is most like the Feudal System?
- Discuss how the Feudal System worked. Draw up a group document that shows the advantages and disadvantages of the system.
- In small groups try to illustrate your decisions about the Feudal System through acting them out.

the importance of king.....2

- Look at the diagram and read the descriptions in the boxes below.
- Try to match each of the 5 people described with one of the empty spaces on the diagram.
- Write in the person's name on the diagram.

'Pyramid' feudal system.

KING   WHO OWNS ALL THE LAND

TENANTS IN CHIEF
KNIGHTS AND BARONS
(ABOUT 200)

BISHOP

UNDER-TENANTS
(ABOUT 8000)

PEASANTS
(ABOUT 1·5 MILLION)

PRIESTS

Sir William Granville
A knight who was recruited by Sir Robert de Bernay to fight for Duke William. A reliable and trusty warrior, who owns a farm in Normandy.

Peter the Peasant
A freeman, but a peasant who does not own any land. He wants to carry on renting from his new landlord.

Sir Robert de Bernay
A powerful nobleman and personal friend of King William. He is a Norman who helped William to raise men and money for his invasion of England. He fought at his side at the Battle of Hastings.

Pierre de Rouen
An ambitious priest recruited by Bishop Odo, Duke William's brother. He is keen to unite the English church to the Norman church, and is a good leader of men.

Eaorl Edgar
Fought against William at Hastings, but decided to surrender in 1067 when William's army came to his area. Hopes desperately to be able to keep some of his land.

---

ordinary life.....1

For the majority of people in England, life was hard and basic.....

The roof overhung the walls to stop them getting too wet. Tiles and slate were only used on very grand buildings, so peasants used straw, turf, wood or thatch.

Walls were often made of WATTLE AND DAUB. Wattle was a woven frame of branches and twigs. This was then 'daubed', or smothered in a mixture of clay, mud, chopped straw and dung. It was allowed to dry thoroughly, and was then whitewashed to keep out the wet. Provided this did not get wet it provided a fairly watertight wall.

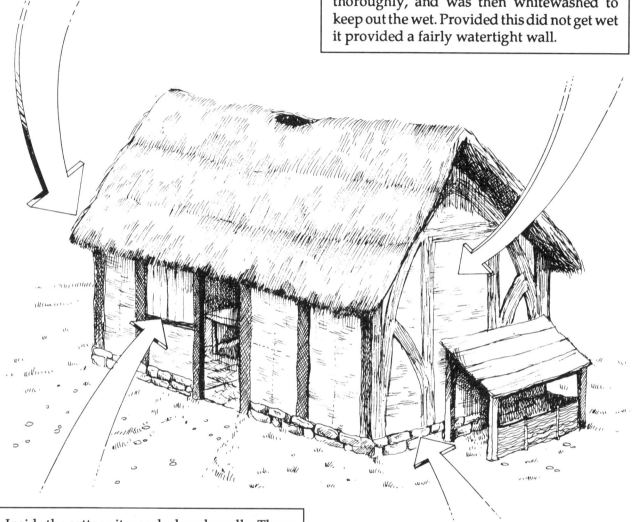

Inside the cottage it was dark and smelly. There was no upstairs, and only one room. Animals would sleep at one end of the room in a pen. This was safe for the animals, and provided warmth. The cooking fire was in the middle of the floor, well away from walls, and there was no chimney. Windows were just holes in the wall, with shutters for night-time.

Houses were homemade using local materials, such as wood, turf and thatch. The walls would be on a low stone base, to stop them from rotting away, but whole houses were made of stone only in a few areas where stone was plentiful.

- Why do you think so few peasants' cottages are still surviving today?
- Write a description of a visit to a cottage like this.
- Make a list comparing your home to a medieval house.

One step further .....

- Using local materials and NO glue, plasticine etc., try to construct your own model of a medieval hut. Although these houses were small and uncomfortable by our standards, they did have some advantages. Try to work out what these were. A CLUE: think of money!

Peasants worked in the communal fields around the village. They also owed their lord (usually a knight or baron) a regular amount of work, or service, in his fields. In return the lord protected them from enemies and administered justice.

In the garden of the cottage the family grew their vegetables and kept their animals. The food they grew here and the grain from the fields had to keep them alive through the year.

SOURCE 1

Birmingham

Richard holds Bermingeham of William (William FitzAnsculf, a tenant-in-chief) ... There is land for 6 ploughs; there is one plough in the demesne (Richard's private land). There are 5 villeins and 4 bordars and 2 ploughs. There is a wood half a mile long and 4 furlongs broad. In the time of King Edward it was worth 20 shillings, and it is still worth the same.

SOURCE 2

Brook in Norfolk

Brook was held by Earl Gyrth in the time of King Edward, and King William gave it to the abbey of St Edmund. There were then 33 villeins; now 38. Then as now 3 slaves. Now 3 ploughs on the demesne and 6 ploughs belonging to the men. Woodland for 30 pigs; 9 acres of meadow. Now 5 horses, 14 beasts, 40 pigs, 65 sheep and 20 goats.

Villeins and bordars were types of peasants.

In 1086 William the Conqueror decided to make a list of all of the property he owned. This really meant a list of the contents of the kingdom. This survey was called the Domesday Book.

The Domesday book was written to a formula. Commissioners were sent out to every village to ask all of the people the same questions. These were then written out in a sort of shorthand to save time. People thought it was like Domesday, or Judgement Day, which is when God will ask everybody what they did with their life.

- Why were most peasants likely to have a knight or baron as their lord?
- Why did William want to know about England in such a lot of detail?
- What do we have today in place of a Domesday Book?

One step further .....

Using the sources, work out for each:
- Who owned it at the start of 1066, and who owns it now.
- How much it was worth then.
- Whether it is richer or poorer now.
- What can historians use this sort of evidence for?

women in society.....1

The vast majority of women were peasants, who with their families belonged to their lord. Women would look after children and spin wool to make thread to sell and weave into clothes for their families.....

These are typical jobs done every day by a woman and the younger children.

1 hour
collecting water

1 hour
cooking and
preparing food

1 hour
collecting fuel for
cooking and heat

1 hour
milking and tending to
animals

1 hour
gardening and collecting
wild berries, roots and
herbs

1 hour
cleaning and washing

The rest of the day would be spent on seasonal tasks, perhaps helping in the fields, weaving, slaughtering an animal, nursing a sick relative or repairing the house.

- Which was the most difficult job? Make a list in order of difficulty, and explain your reasons.
- Why do you think cleaning and washing took so little time?
- What did all of the other tasks have in common? Why was this so important?

One step further .....

- Make up a timetable for a typical woman's day.
- Compare your timetable with the day of a woman you know well, perhaps your mum.
- What are the main differences? What are the similarities?

Women had few rights in society. A girl was the property of her father, and when she married she became her husband's property. The only women who were free from this control were widows. There was no divorce.

A girl who chose to remain unmarried might go into a nunnery, which meant that she would have her life controlled by the church. A girl who remained unmarried and at home was a disgrace to her family, and could not help them financially except through spinning.

Most men also had a very low status as peasants who belonged to their lord, so the even worse position of women did not seem so bad as it might today. A woman had almost the same status as an animal, except that she could not be killed. A wife who was injured in a fight might have compensation paid to her husband, as she was not meant to own property. A passage from the Bible was used as the reason for this:

Wives, submit to your husbands as to the Lord. For a husband has authority over his wife just as Christ has authority over the church ....

What is surprising in the Middle Ages is that the vast majority of women seem to have enjoyed their lives, instead of being miserable.

- Find out what the name is for an unmarried woman.
- How was the passage from the Bible used to justify women's position in society?
- Why was it important to have lots of children in medieval times?
- How would this keep women in a subservient position?

One step further .....

- Were women stupid in not standing up for their rights? Discuss this in groups, and then make up your own play to explain why women could not rebel.

courts and punishments.....1

There was no prison system in the Middle Ages and crimes were punished in different ways.....

Some crimes were obvious, such as murder, robbery or assault. A serious crime was tried at a county court by a judge. Twelve men had to give evidence about the crime and the character of the person accused, and then the judge decided if the accused was guilty or not.

To help to keep law and order men over twelve were sometimes part of a TYTHING system. Groups of ten men had to keep an eye on each other, and their leader had to report on any misbehaviour to the county sheriff at a special court held every six months. This system got too difficult to administer, and gradually died out by about 1400.

Law and order was kept by villagers or townspeople themselves. In small communities it was difficult to commit a crime and get away with it. When the lord or baron (or his steward) visited the village he would listen to the wrongdoings and decide on punishments.

A CONSTABLE was chosen by a village to keep order during daylight. Towns would sometimes employ a constable, but most had to do their own work as well. It was an unpopular and thankless job, so most constables did it very badly in the hope that they wouldn't have to do it again.

HUE AND CRY simply meant that anyone who saw a crime being committed had a duty to shout it out and chase the criminal. If they didn't do this, the witness could also be punished. This was a very effective way of stopping crime, if it was witnessed.

At night in towns there was a CURFEW. This meant a bell was rung, and all honest people were meant to stay indoors. Sometimes a group of men would patrol the streets, they were called the WATCH. All men had to take their turn in the watch, but because this meant losing a night's sleep the watch didn't do a very good job. There were no street lights, so it was easy for criminals to escape.

- What do you think was the most effective way of keeping law and order in medieval times?
- Why was it very difficult to prove who had committed a crime?
- Whose final responsibility was law and order?
- Why was a person's reputation and character so important?

One step further .....

- For each method of keeping law and order, make a list of the good and bad points.
- Make up a dramatic scene in which a criminal is caught using one of these methods.

There was no prison system in the Middle Ages. The most serious crimes were punished by death, and people accused of serious crimes were kept in the dungeons of the nearest lord until their trial.

Other punishments relied on humiliation. Drunks would be put in the pillory or stocks, where people could laugh at them. Someone who sold bad goods would be dragged round the town on a hurdle (gate), with the bad goods displayed. A baker might be forced to eat his mouldy bread, a wineseller might have to drink his bad wine.

Women could be ducked in a pond, or were made to wear a special bridle to hold their tongue still, if they were accused of trying to boss their husband. They might have their hair shaved off if they got too concerned for their appearance.

The most common punishment was a fine of money or goods. This was paid to the person who was wronged, or to the court.

People who offended against the church laws had to perform a public penance. They might have to walk barefoot, or even on their knees, to church. Perhaps they would have to confess their wrongdoing to the whole congregation in church.

Criminals could also be mutilated. They might be beaten or flogged, this was a punishment for persistent beggars. They might have their cheek or hand branded with the initial of their crime, or a hole bored through their ear. Ears, noses, hands and feet might be chopped off.

These punishments seem unfair, sexist and harsh. But English justice was famous all over the world, because there was no punishment without trial.

- Why were there no prisons in the Middle Ages?
- Fines were very commonly used as a punishment. Why was this a good idea?
- What was the point of humiliating a criminal? What did this try to do?
- What was the point of mutilation? How might this stop crime?

One step further .....

- Hangings and beheadings were public entertainment in medieval times. Why do you think the public were encouraged to take an active role in punishing criminals?
- Do you agree with punishments like mutilation and hanging? You might like to organise a class debate on the reasons for this type of punishment, and whether it works.
- English justice was famous all over the world. What does this tell you about the systems of justice in other countries?

wool.....1

There were not enough people to grow crops all over England, so the areas between villages remained woodland. But this wood was gradually used by the villagers .....

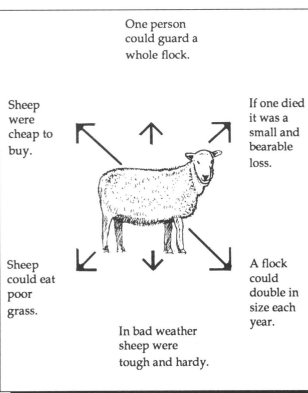

One person could guard a whole flock.

Sheep were cheap to buy.

If one died it was a small and bearable loss.

Sheep could eat poor grass.

A flock could double in size each year.

In bad weather sheep were tough and hardy.

The land left by cutting down the forests was too rough to plough, and so sheep were kept there. Sheep had several advantages over other domestic animals.

After the Black Death had hit England the population was cut by between a third and a half. Sheep farming was already successful, and many landlords changed to sheep farming, which needed fewer people.

- What do you think the woods were used for?
- Find out how mutton (sheep meat) was preserved for the winter.
- Using the picture, work out why the new land was unusable. Then try to design your own alternative use for this land.

One step further .....

- Sheep also produce many things to eat, drink, wear or sell. Make your own sheep diagram to show the products of sheep.
- Find out about some of the breeds of English sheep. Most are named after areas of England. Why do you think this is?

The main product from sheep was wool. Every year each fleece produced enough wool to knit three jumpers. English wool was meant to be the best in the world, and peasants could sell their surplus to merchants who travelled around the country.

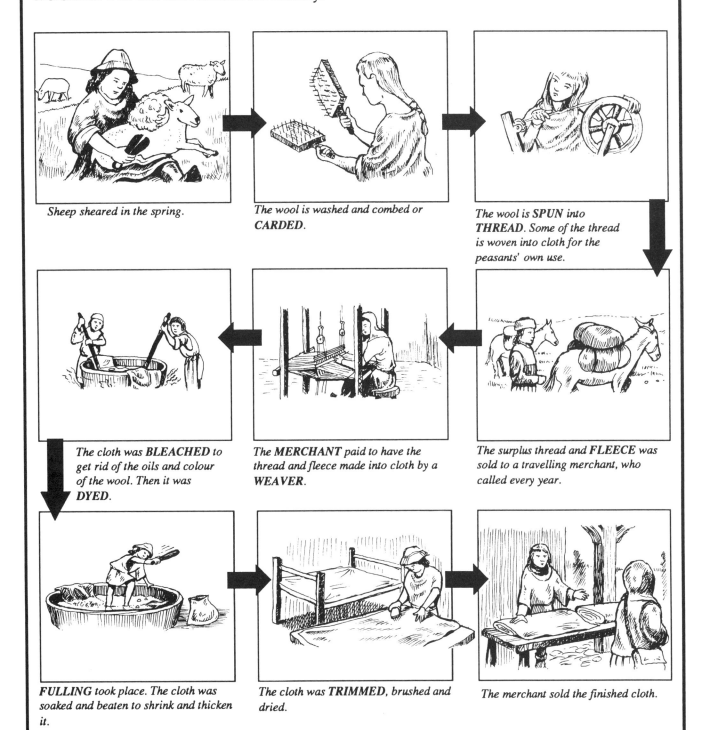

Sheep sheared in the spring.

The wool is washed and combed or **CARDED**.

The wool is **SPUN** *into* **THREAD**. *Some of the thread is woven into cloth for the peasants' own use.*

The cloth was **BLEACHED** *to get rid of the oils and colour of the wool. Then it was* **DYED**.

The **MERCHANT** *paid to have the thread and fleece made into cloth by a* **WEAVER**.

The surplus thread and **FLEECE** *was sold to a travelling merchant, who called every year.*

FULLING *took place. The cloth was soaked and beaten to shrink and thicken it.*

The cloth was **TRIMMED**, *brushed and dried.*

The merchant sold the finished cloth.

- This system of production is called a 'domestic system'. Can you think of reasons for this name?
- What are some of the problems that might occur in this type of production?
- Make a list of the processes wool goes through to become cloth. Check you know what each word means.

One step further .....

- If you were a wealthy merchant, how could you improve on this system? Would there be any new problems as a result of your changes?
- Find out how cloth is produced today. Make a chart or wall display comparing the methods of production.

medieval trade.....1

Charters and markets; guilds and apprentices.....

Public meetings of any kind were not allowed without permission, so it was a great honour to be given a CHARTER. This gave your town official recognition, and permission for a regular market or fair. The king might give your town a charter as a thank-you, or because you had paid for it.

A fair held once or twice a year, or a regular market held every week or month, encouraged people to come to your town to buy or sell goods. This brought wealth to the town. The council could rent out market stalls, or charge a fee for every animal sold. People from the town could rent rooms to the visitors, and sell them food.

A regular market would attract more people to live in the town. They would move in, in order to sell their goods to more people, and would pay taxes to the council. Newcomers could also be made to pay taxes when they built new houses.

Gradually a pattern grew up. In 1066 most people who lived in towns had also grown most of their own food, and had owed service to a lord. By about 1400 townspeople usually had no lord, and had their own town walls for defence. They bought their food from the country people, who travelled into town to sell at the market. Townspeople were craftsmen or servants, and were no longer directly connected with the land.

- What were the advantages of living in a town?
- What were the disadvantages of living in a town?
- What types of people would want to live in a town?

One step further .....

Some towns failed despite having charters or fairs.

- Can you think of some reasons why a town might not grow?
- Towns grew up for a reason. Perhaps they were built near an abbey, or were by a river ford. Think of as many reasons as you can for a town to develop.
- Try to find out if your town developed in the Middle Ages, and why.

medieval trade.....2

At fourteen a boy would be APPRENTICED to a trade. His parents paid a fee to a master craftsman, who would train the boy in his craft. Girls could not become apprentices, but they might be sent to live away from home to learn to be good wives!

The apprentice lived with his master as one of the family. He could not leave without breaking the law. He was not paid.

The apprentice was taught all about the trade, and did the labouring jobs for his master.

After a year and a day he became a freeman of the town, which gave him the right to remain there.

After seven years the apprentice made his MASTERPIECE. This was like taking an exam.

The masterpiece was examined by all the other craftsmen. If it was good enough he could become a master craftsman. If not, he became a JOURNEYMAN, who worked for wages.

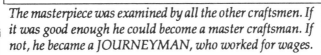

To become a master, the journeyman had to pay a large fee to the GUILD. This was a sort of union, that regulated wages and checked standards of work for each trade. Only masters could belong.

Many journeymen could never afford to join a guild. The guilds became extremely rich, but they also provided sick payments, pensions and schools for guild members and their families.

Journeymen could not take on apprentices. They may have to pay a fee to the guild to sell goods in the town. Or they may have to work under the direction of a master.

- Why were girls not allowed to become apprentices? (Look again at women in society.)
- What type of parents did a boy have to have to become an apprentice?
- Why did apprentices get no wages?
- Why was it very unusual for an apprentice to give up his apprenticeship?

One step further .....

- The work of guildsmen was meant to be the best there was. How did a guildsman make sure his customers knew he had made an article?
- There were many more journeymen than guildsmen, or master craftsmen. Did this mean the work of journeymen was inferior?
- Women could not become journeymen or craftsmen, but many of them worked at their husband's trade, or ran their own shops. What advantages and disadvantages were there for customers in buying goods made by a woman?

daily life.....1

The most important thing in daily life in medieval times was food. Country people grew their own food, and took the surplus to market, where it was bought by town people.....

The main crop was grain. The sort of grain you grew depended where you lived. Wheat, barley, rye and oats were common grains, and these would be ground into flour and made into bread or 'cakes'.

Pulses, like beans and peas, formed an important part of the diet. These would be boiled in a sort of stew, called 'pottage'. Vegetables, leaves and seeds were added for more flavour.

Meat was scarce for most people. From autumn to Christmas surplus livestock was slaughtered, and people would feast on the meat while it was fresh. But meat was so expensive that many peasants might only taste it once a year.

All food had to be dried, smoked or salted to keep it through the winter, and it wasn't until about May that the first crops were ready to be picked and eaten. People would go hungry, and in a bad year with a poor harvest the young children and old people might die. If the harvest failed due to disease or the weather, there would be a famine.

Food was very boring. The rich could afford to buy spices like pepper to help to hide the taste of meat that was rotten, and strong sauces were popular. But for most people the struggle to grow enough to stay alive was all that mattered.

- Design a menu for a medieval peasant family. Remember, everything had to be cooked in a pot over an open fire, or on a hot stone.
- What did the peasants use for sweetening?
- The peasants could not trap game like pigeons or rabbits. Who did these belong to?
- Some peasants ate their seed-corn or vegetables to stay alive in a famine. What would happen to them as a result?

One step further .....

- In a poor year, the peasants would eat anything they could find growing. This might include beech leaves or grass! Find out as many foods as you can that are edible and grow wild in this country.
- Fortunately famines in England tended to come only about every ten years, and were usually local. What welfare agencies existed to help people who were starving?

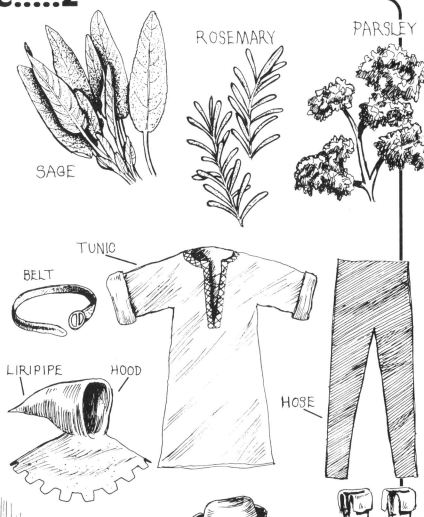

Herbs were plants that grew wild or were cultivated in gardens. They were very important, both as a flavouring for food, and as a medicine. Only the very rich could afford a doctor, and even doctors used a mixture of herb medicine and 'magic' for their patients.

In medieval times there was little understanding of what caused disease, and the importance of hygiene. So every village would have a woman who understood herbal remedies and helped the other women when they had babies or their families were sick. This woman was often known as GOODWIFE. She was not paid, but was often an older woman whose own family had grown up.

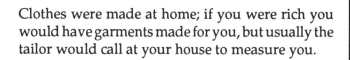

Clothes were made at home; if you were rich you would have garments made for you, but usually the tailor would call at your house to measure you.

Simple cloth could be made at home, but it was easier to buy it at market. Then the cloth would be sewn by the women of the family into clothes. The style was simple and basic, and relied on layers for warmth. Due to the expense, time and trouble in making clothes, most peasants only had one set of garments. These might be inherited second-hand, and would have to be worn until they fell apart. Even then the rags would be used as patches or padding.

- Why did people not understand about germs in the Middle Ages?
- Why was fashion unimportant to most medieval people?
- Why was it easier, and often cheaper, to buy material than to make it at home?

One step further .....

- Goodwives were not medically trained. Did this mean that their help was useless?
- Herbal cures are still in common use today. Try to find out some of them.
- The average life expectancy for a medieval person was less than forty years. When was the most risky time of a person's life?

When William I became king in 1066, he had given about a quarter of his kingdom to the church. He believed that God had helped him to win his kingdom, and this was his way of giving thanks.....

The church land was not all in one place. In every town or village that had a church, the land the church was built on and the building now belonged to the church, and not the local baron. Large areas of land in the North of England were given to monasteries, to farm and to settle.

Priests who ran the local churches owed obedience and service to the BISHOP, who was in charge of a large area. The bishop ran church courts in the same way as a lord running a manor court. The difference was that the bishop administered church or CANON law, instead of the ordinary laws.

- Draw your own diagram to show how the church was governed. You may like to look at the diagram of the Feudal System to give yourself the idea.
- Do you think that the peasants who worked on church lands had an easier life? Give reasons for your answer.
- What would be the biggest and strongest building in most villages? Why?

The church also collected its own tax, called a TITHE. Tithe means tenth. Everybody had to pay a tenth part of their produce or earnings to the church every year. This money was used to support the priest and church. Surplus goods were stored in a 'Tithe Barn', and sold to raise more money or given to charity. The bishop and his court and palace also claimed a share of this tax. A regular amount was paid to the POPE in Rome. This was because the whole church was governed from Rome in Italy, and the pope was the leader of the church who lived in Rome.

Where did the TITHE go?

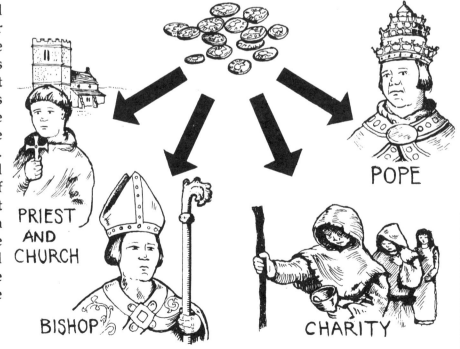

PRIEST AND CHURCH

POPE

BISHOP

CHARITY

One step further .....

- What difficulties might arise from having the leader of the church in another country?
- Try to find out how the Church of England is administered today. Who is your local bishop?
- Why do you think the idea of paying tithes has died out?

Bishops were often criticised for their power and wealth, which was not very Christ-like. But throughout the Middle Ages there were examples of churchmen who tried to do their best for God and the church.

Bishop Odo

Odo was the half-brother of William I, and had helped him in the Battle of Hastings. Odo is likely to have ordered the Bayeux Tapestry to be made, as he is shown frequently. He carried a club into battle, and not a sword, because he was a man of God! Odo probably influenced William into giving such a large part of his new kingdom to the church.

Under the Normans many new priests and bishops were appointed from Normandy, and they set about rebuilding the old Saxon churches in the Norman style. This is still important today, as many of our churches were first built by the Normans.

Thomas Becket

King Henry II (1154-1189) tried to limit the powers of the church courts. Many dangerous criminals were escaping justice by claiming to be members of the CLERGY (churchmen). Henry appointed his best friend, Thomas Becket, to be Archbishop of Canterbury, in the belief that he would help him.

Thomas changed when he was archbishop. He became very holy and refused to do anything that would harm the power of the church. In a fit of anger Henry wished Thomas was dead, and four of his knights thought this was a command. Thomas was hacked to death in Canterbury Cathedral, and became a world-famous saint. Henry was heartbroken, and unable to do any more about reforming the church, which remained powerful until 1534.

John Wycliffe

John Wycliffe lived in the fourteenth century, when the church was getting increasingly wealthy and powerful. He urged Christians to give up wealth and riches and live as simply as Christ; particularly the bishops who should set an example.

Wycliffe was also concerned that the Bible and church teaching were in Latin, which meant only the educated could understand the word of God. He and his friends made the first English translation of the Bible in 1382. Wycliffe died in 1384, but his ideas lived on, until finally the church was reformed 150 years later.

- Why would Odo want lots of pictures showing himself in the Bayeux Tapestry?
- Why was Henry II so angry when Thomas Becket would not obey his commands?
- Were Wycliffe's ideas practical and realistic? What did he hope churchmen would do when they heard him?

Life was not secure in Medieval England. People were used to death in a way that we are not today.....

Every year there was the possibility of famine. If someone was sick, they would be nursed at home. Disease was difficult to cure as there were few effective medicines. Many young children died each year from diseases such as measles. Simple accidents, such as cuts or a broken arm, might lead to death through infection.

There was also the risk that your lord would involve you in a war. If he decided to put up your rent to pay soldiers, you might starve. He might order the men of the village to go and fight, which would make planting enough crops very difficult. If fighting between two lords took place near your village, your food would be taken, and perhaps homes burned and villagers killed.

Due to the nearness of death, people were aware of what happened to them after they died in a way that we are not today. They believed that if they went to church and lived a good life they would go to HEAVEN. But if they lived a bad life, then they would go to HELL.

The church encouraged these beliefs by wall paintings and stained-glass pictures that showed JUDGEMENT DAY. This was when God would judge everybody according to how they had lived. Priests wanted people to live good, peaceful lives, and to support the work of the church through gifts, so they encouraged this belief.

- Find out what people believed Heaven and Hell were like.
- How did they believe they could escape going to Hell?
- Give some examples that a priest might have used to show a good life.

One step further .....

- Vivid pictures were painted in some churches showing Judgement Day or Domesday. Try drawing your own version of one of these pictures.
- Why do you think people today are much less concerned about Heaven and Hell?

beliefs and the church.....2

Most people could not read or write so they relied on the priest to tell them what God wanted them to do. Gradually, from 1066 until about 1530, the church came to give its own ideas about how people should behave, rather than keeping to the ideas in the Bible.

There were some attempts to return to a more Christian way of life. People like John Wycliffe, John Ball and the founders of the monasteries, tried to simplify the church and give away some of its wealth, but many of the rich church leaders objected. All through the Middle Ages groups of reformers tried, unsuccessfully, to make the church less wealthy.

The church also had its own laws. Henry II had tried to control these laws and failed. Gradually people grew tired of the power of the church courts. This was because they grew far more lax than the ordinary courts. For example, there was no death penalty, even for murder. Ordinary people might have to perform a humiliating punishment for the church court, but the rich and churchmen might be let off with a fine for the same offence. All a man had to do to be tried by a church court was to recite the Lord's Prayer in Latin, so many people escaped the king's justice.

But the church was also popular, and performed many good works (welfare). Everybody had to go to church, so it is not surprising that some were evil men who gave the church a bad name. Most ordinary priests were good men who worked hard to look after the people in their village, and were not interested in getting rich. During a time when the future was uncertain, the church gave hope and help to millions of people.

- Complete the diagram to show the good and bad points about the church.
- List as many ways as you can to show how the church was involved in everyday life.
- What was unfair about Canon (church) law?

GOOD POINTS	BAD POINTS

One step further .....

- You are living in 1400. Write a letter to a friend explaining the influence that the church has on your life.
- How could the power of the church affect the power of the king?

The Church and Society.....

Some men and women in medieval England did not want to live normal lives, get married and live in society. They might choose instead to give their lives to God and the service of other people. This meant they joined a MONASTERY.

A monastery, or abbey, was a community of men or women who spent their lives in good works and prayer. When a monk joined the abbey he made three promises. These were POVERTY, CHASTITY and OBEDIENCE. He must own nothing, have no sexual relationships, and obey the rules of his abbey without question. A monk earned no wages, but worked for his abbey for free.

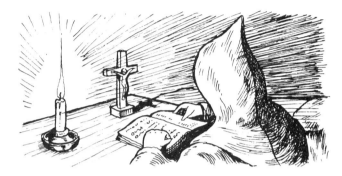

- Why do you think the three promises had to be made by every monk?
- Explain why a monk had to learn to obey orders without question.
- Why might men and women choose to be monks or nuns? Make a list of the reasons.

Monasteries were not all the same; different types or ORDERS had been founded by different leaders. But all existed to glorify God. Some, like the Benedictines, were in towns, but the Cistercians had reclaimed wasteland in Wales and the north. There were also groups called FRIARS, who travelled around the country, but had a monastery as a base.

A monk had to work hard. There were regular church services all through the day and night, a time of learning and prayer, and about six hours of work a day. Punishment was harsh for monks who broke any rules.

Although monks were not allowed to own anything, their monasteries grew very wealthy. This was because ordinary people saw and admired the work the monks did, and gave them presents of money and goods. Rich men would leave money to the monasteries in their will. The monks spent a lot of money on charity, and also rebuilt and extended their monasteries, but could not always spend all they were given.

One step further .....

- Why did people start to criticise the monasteries as time went on?
- Find out about some of the different ORDERS of monks. What did they do and wear that made them different from each other?
- Monasteries owned land all over England. Find out if land near you was owned by monks at some time, and whether they lived locally or far away.
- How did monks justify owning property with their rule of poverty?

The monks provided many of the welfare services that the council looks after today. Before the monks no one had provided these, so the local population was very grateful.

Hospitals for the sick and terminally ill. Everyone could use these hospitals, but they were particularly useful for those who had no family.

Accommodation for travellers. Anyone could stay at a monastery overnight, without running the risk of being robbed through having to sleep rough, or in a strange house. Travel was slow and dangerous, so there were not many inns.

Education was given to boys who lived locally. Sometimes the boys were expected to enter the monastery, but not always.

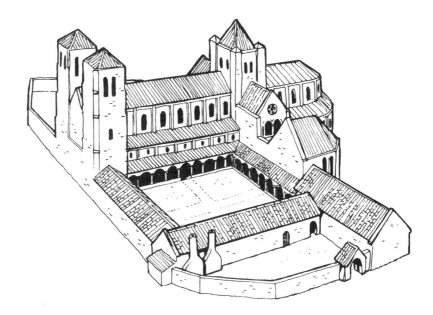

Books were kept in monastic libraries. In the time before printing was invented, only monks had the time and education to copy out books by hand.

Monks acted as clerks and administrators, even to the king. Only churchmen had the time and opportunity to learn to read and write.

Monks cared for the old, either in the monastery itself, or in specially built cottages nearby.

In times of famine or disease the monks did their best to look after the people in the surrounding area.

● Make a list of the way that councils look after all of these things today.
● Everyone who worked in a monastery was called a monk. What title would we give to people doing these jobs today?
● As the Middle Ages progressed, these welfare jobs changed. See if you can work out which became more important and which became less as time went on.

One step further .....

● Imagine you are a boy who has just entered a monastery. Write a letter to a friend describing some of the jobs you are hoping to do.
● Everybody in a monastery lived to a strict timetable. Find out the timetable for one monastery - they were each slightly different.
● How do people today get their training for jobs?

Magna Carta.....1

William I gave his followers land, which they divided up among their knights or barons.....

At first the barons were controlled by strong kings, but by 1150 they were fighting wars against each other for more territory, and building castles without permission from the king. This made life very hard for the ordinary people.

Henry II (1154-1189) was another strong king, and he forced the barons to obey him and destroyed their illegal castles. But after he died the barons gradually wanted more power again.

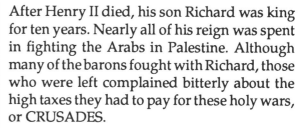

After Henry II died, his son Richard was king for ten years. Nearly all of his reign was spent in fighting the Arabs in Palestine. Although many of the barons fought with Richard, those who were left complained bitterly about the high taxes they had to pay for these holy wars, or CRUSADES.

John, Richard's younger brother, inherited the throne in 1199. He was already unpopular as he disliked fighting, but had collected Richard's taxes. Now John had to put taxes up again to pay for wars against the French king, who took many of England's territories in France. In these wars John had had his nephew Arthur murdered when he was a prisoner, and he failed to win back the English lands.

- Why were barons not allowed to build castles without permission?
- How were the lives of ordinary people affected by baronial wars?
- Why was King Richard a popular king, even though he spent less than a year of his reign in England?

John had also quarrelled with the Pope. He claimed that he could appoint his own Archbishop of Canterbury, but the Pope refused to allow this. As a result, England was under an INTERDICT from 1208 to 1213. This meant there could be no services held in English churches, which cut off all the people of England from God.

In 1213 John gave in to the Pope, and paid a huge fine. Stephen Langton became Archbishop of Canterbury. John was now very unpopular with the barons, who saw him as godless, grasping and a failure. In 1214 John's barons joined together against him, and marched to London.

One step further .....

- Why was King John such an unpopular king with (a) the barons, and (b) the peasants?
- Draw a cartoon version of John's life.
- The Robin Hood legend grew up at this time. See if you can think of reasons for the start of this legend, and its popularity.

The barons did not want to get rid of John, but they wanted to force him to obey certain rules to make him a better king. They were united by Stephen Langton, the new Archbishop of Canterbury. Langton realised that it would not benefit the kingdom if John was executed, because the barons would just continue to fight against each other.

Langton and the barons drew up a list of grievances, and a GREAT CHARTER, or document, which set them right. This is what MAGNA CARTA means. Magna Carta set out the 'customs of the realm' in Henry II's reign, and said that John should not try to change the customs by which the kingdom was governed. Justice was also given to everyone - John had been charging people for going to court! Fines were fixed, again John had been charging rich people more.

Magna Carta really was to guard the power of the barons. John was forced to sign it at Runnymede, near Windsor, on 15th June 1215. But as soon as he could, he escaped from the barons and began to fight against them. However, he died in 1216.

Henry III succeeded John. He was a weak king, and in 1258 the Earl of Leicester, Simon de Montfort took over government. He governed the kingdom with a council of fifteen barons. From 1264 to 1265 a great council governed the country. As well as the powerful lords, this included two knights chosen from every shire, city and borough, and was the first parliament.

Henry's eldest son Edward fought against de Montfort, and killed him in 1265. However, when Edward became king in 1272, he also used the idea of parliament. Edward I's first Parliament was in 1275.

After this time kings called regular parliaments. They did not make laws, but gave the king advice and told him what people throughout the country were thinking. They were useful in telling the people what the king had decided to do, and explaining his reasons.

- Who was the most important influence in drawing up Magna Carta?
- What might the barons have tried to do instead?
- Why do you think the charter had a Latin name?
- The word PARLIAMENT is also foreign, from the French word PARLER. What does this word mean?

One step further .....

- John was also unpopular with the peasants. Why was it only possible for the barons to stand up to him?
- Magna Carta was copied out and sent to every important town in England. Why was this done?
- How did having a parliament help the king? Who had advised him before?
- Ordinary people could not go to Parliament or help choose who went. Did this mean parliament was useless for most people?

wars.....1

Relations between England and Wales...

WALES

Wales was a separate country from England, and divided into tribes, each with their own prince or ruler. The tribes fought among themselves and sometimes invaded the English border. To stop this the Norman kings built a series of castles along the border or MARCHES. Gradually the influence of the powerful English lords extended into Wales.

In the thirteenth century the Welsh, under Llewellyn the Great, took back their land from the English. In 1276 Llewellyn's grandson, also Llewellyn, led a revolt against the authority of the English in Wales. The English king, Edward I, fought a war against the Welsh for seven years. At the end of that time he forced the Welsh to submit to English rule.

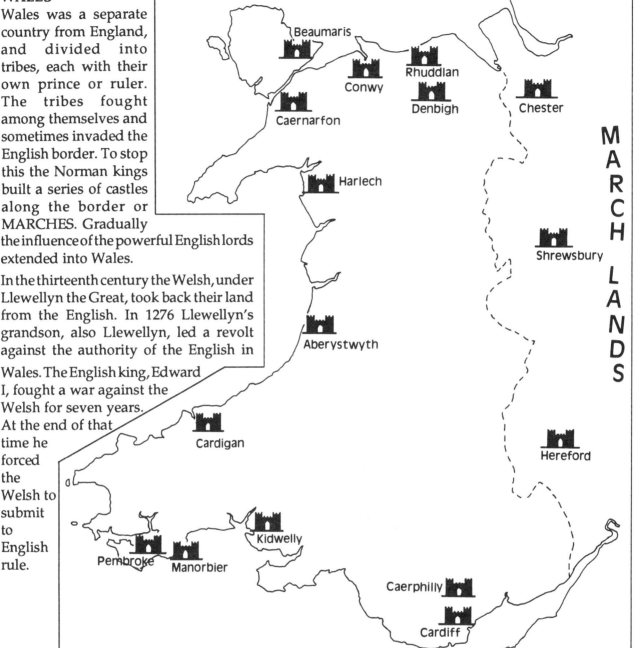

Wales was divided into counties, and English laws were introduced. Castles were built as strongholds of English rule. But Edward allowed the Welsh to keep some of their laws and customs, and their own language. He also made his eldest son the Prince of Wales.

- Why did the Welsh not try to invade England?
- The Welsh traded with the English. How did this help Edward I to invade?
- Why was it important for Edward to leave the Welsh their customs and language?
- How did this make the Welsh easy to control?

One step further .....

- Llewellyn the Great took back Welsh lands from the March lords. What authority did the English still have in Wales?
- What was the significance of making Edward's baby son the Prince of Wales?
- Edward's new castles were built by deep rivers or on the coast. Why was this important? What was he prepared for?

wars.....2

... and England and Scotland.....

SCOTLAND

Scotland was also a separate country from England, but in 1286 the king of Scotland died, leaving the throne to his three-year-old granddaughter, who lived in Norway. The little girl died on her way to Scotland, and the Scots appealed to Edward I to help them decide on a new king.

Edward chose a man called Balliol to be king in 1292. Balliol was known to be sympathetic to England, but the idea of being king changed him and he rebelled against Edward in 1296. Edward captured Balliol, and took him to London.

In 1297 a Scottish nobleman called William Wallace led the Scottish nobles against Edward's army, and defeated them at Stirling. But in 1298 the Scots were beaten at Falkirk. Wallace then led the Scots in a successful GUERILLA war against the English.

Wallace was betrayed, captured and executed in 1305, but the Scots were determined not to submit to the English and crowned Robert Bruce king at Scone in 1306. Edward I marched north to defeat the new king, but died in 1307. Edward's son, Edward II, tried to defeat the Scots, but was beaten at Bannockburn in 1314. After that Scotland continued as an independent country until 1603.

- The Scots and English did not trade very much. How did this affect Edward's attempts to take over Scotland?
- Why did Edward choose Balliol as king?
- What is a guerilla war? Why was it successful against the English?
- Edward I is sometimes called 'The Hammer of the Scots'. What does this mean? Is this a fair name?

One step further .....

- There were several Scottish leaders who fought against Edward. What did this show about the attitude of the Scots to the English?
- What advantages did the Scots have in resisting the English?
- Draw a cartoon version of Edward I's campaigns in Scotland. You could use a different background colour to show whether the Scots and English were successful in each picture.

100 years war and warfare.....1

The Hundred Years War did not really lcst for 100 years! In fact there was occasional fighting in France between 1337 and 1453.....

King John had lost most of the English lands in France, but King Edward III claimed that he had the right to the French throne, and declared war in 1337. This was also partly to occupy the barons, to win popularity and to protect English traders who were threatened by the French.

1340 Battle of Sluys. The first big sea battle to be won by the English.

1346 Battle of Crecy. Won by the English.

1356 Battle of Poitiers. Won by the English.

1360 Treaty of Bretigny. This kept the peace until 1369. Edward agreed to give up his claim to the French throne, and possessions owned by Henry II. In return he kept all other English possessions, including those he had just won.

1372 Battle of Rochelle. The English fleet were defeated.

1374 The English only kept Calais, Bordeaux and Bayonne. The French had won back everything else.

1396 A new truce was made when Richard II married the sister of the French king.

1415 Henry V (1413-22) decided to claim the throne of France. He landed near Harfleur in northern France and captured the town.

1415 Battle of Agincourt. Won by the English, who then had to return to England for reinforcements.

1417 The English reinvaded northern France.

1420 Treaty of Troyes. Henry married the French princess and became the heir to the French throne. He died in 1422 before becoming king of France.

1428-9 Siege of Orleans. The English besieged Orleans. The French, led by Joan of Arc, drove the English out.

1429-1453 The English found it difficult to pay for wars in France, and there were no more attempts at invasion. In 1445 Henry VI married Margaret of Anjou, and this helped to make peace. By 1450 the English had lost all of their territory in Northern France, except for Calais.

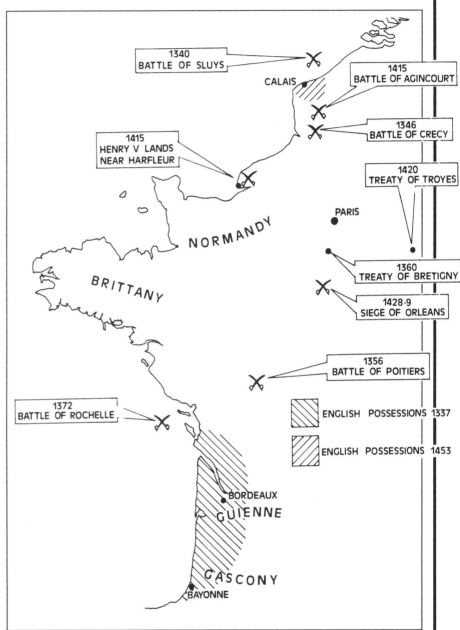

- Make a timeline for the Hundred Years War.
- Make a list of the different reasons given by the English for invading France.
- Give each reason a mark out of ten for whether it was a good or bad reason.

One step further .....

- Use the section on the Feudal System to help you in discovering how the kings of England raised an army to fight in France.
- How would this method of recruiting an army have to change in a long war?
- Some men would be prepared to fight for no wages at all. How would they hope to get a reward?
- What is the name we use today for soldiers who will fight for anybody, provided they get paid?

100 years war and warfare.....2

The armies of medieval England relied on three main types of fighting men.

Archers were the main force of the English army. All men were meant to practise with the longbow every week after church. They wore light armour, and relied on firing up to twelve arrows every minute to protect themselves. No other country used the longbow to such an extent.

Spearmen/pikemen were a newer development. They came close to the enemy and fought them hand to hand with swords or spears. Pikes were very long, heavy spears that were sometimes 'planted' in front of archers to give them protection from mounted soldiers.

Knights were heavily armed and armoured. At first their armour was for protection, but it gradually got so heavy that it was impossible for a knight to dress himself in it, or to fight effectively. English knights tended to wear lighter armour in battle, and to fight on foot. The French knights remained fully armoured. This meant they had to fight on horseback, and if they fell off they might suffocate, and could not defend themselves. This weakness accounted for the French defeats at Crecy and Agincourt.

COATS OF ARMS

When a man was wearing armour it was hard to recognise who he was, or which side he was on. So foot soldiers would wear a badge, and a knight would have his coat of arms embroidered on his surcoat, and painted on his shield. The coat of arms, or heraldic emblem was given by the king. It might be a reference to the knight's name or place of birth. A man called Fisher might have an emblem of a fish! All of the men under the command of that knight wore his emblem.

- Individuals fighting each other were rare early in a battle. Explain why.
- What advantages did a knight on horseback have?
- What advantages did a knight on foot have?
- Early armour was made of lots of links, called chain mail. Later it was made of steel plates joined with leather straps. Why was this later armour more effective?

One step further .....

- Design your own coat of arms. If possible it should have a reference to your name, or something to do with you.
- Find out the coat of arms of your nearest town. Make a copy of it.
- See if you can draw and label a suit of armour. Each individual piece had its own name.
- Knights practised fighting at tournaments. Why do you think these were at their most popular during the Hundred Years War?

the black death.....1

The Black Death was not understood very well at the time. People thought that it was caused by poisoned water or bad air. Some people feared it was a plot by Jews to kill Christians.....

This is how the disease spread.

The plague germ lived in the blood of animals, particularly the 'Plague Flea'. Fleas lived in the fur and hair of animals, particularly the black rat.

Fleas live by biting their carriers to suck out a drop of blood. At the same time the germ entered the skin of the animal, which might then catch the disease.

Fleas cannot move far. But the black rats they lived on could travel longer distances. Gradually the rats spread the plague from town to town, and country to country.

People were not very concerned about hygiene, and did not have spare clothes. Houses had thatched roofs and straw on the floor for warmth. Most animals and people had fleas or nits because of this.

Although the Black Death (1348-49) was probably the worst ever natural disaster, killing about a third to a half of the entire population, the plague did not die out. Outbreaks continued about every ten years until better living conditions cleaned up the cities in about 1700.

We have only found out within the last 150 years what actually caused the Black Death. The invention of powerful microscopes has enabled us to see the germ; something medieval people had no chance of doing.

Plague outbreaks continue even today. The plague affects places where hygiene is poor, the conditions are hot and people live close together. It can be treated with modern drugs.

- What is a PLAGUE?
- Explain how a lack of hygiene helped to spread the plague.
- Why did people at the time not understand how the disease was spread?
- What types of houses were less likely to become infected with the Black Death?

One step further .....

- Explain why there are so few written accounts of the Black Death.
- Make a list of the ways that people might react to the news that the Black Death was in their area.
- Make up your own story or drama about the Black Death to show the reactions of ordinary people to the disease. Remember that between a third and a half of the people died.
- Make up a newspaper about the Black Death coming to your town in 1349.

In 1348 there were actually two sorts of plague, both carried around at the same time. This is what made the death total so high.

PNEUMONIC PLAGUE

This could be caught by inhaling the breath of an infected person, as well as through being bitten by a plague flea. It affected the lungs. They filled up with a yellowish-green pus, and the person died from being unable to cough this away. Death was usually very quick, within 24 hours of catching the disease.

BUBONIC PLAGUE

This is where the plague got it's name 'Black Death'. This could only be caught from a flea bite, although people at the time did not know this.

Day 1: Runny nose, sore throat and headache.

Day 2: Very bad headache and fever. Difficulty swallowing.

Day 3: Red swellings come up under the arms, on the neck and at the tops of the thighs.

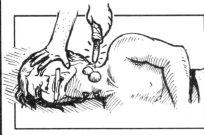

Day 4: The swellings continue to grow, up to the size of a tennis ball. They are filled with pus. As they grow the blood vessels rupture around them and the pain is intense. Some doctors tried to CAUTERISE or burn away the swellings with a red hot poker.

Day 5: The swellings had turned black and hard. The patient usually died in agony.

Day 6: Some patients began to recover. They remained in a lot of pain and very weak for several months. The swellings gradually went down and disappeared.

- Where does the name 'Black Death' come from?
- Some people recovered from the Bubonic Plague. Why were they still likely to die even after this?
- What common ailment is this disease similar to until day 3?

One step further .....

- Why don't we even know how many people died of the Black Death?
- Many priests thought the Black Death was a curse from God. Why might they think this?
- What precautions could have been taken against catching the disease? Why did so few of them work?

society changes.....1

After the Black Death in 1348-9, nothing was ever the same. Between a third and a half of the people in England had died. Many of those who were left were permanently weakened by the disease.....

Some villages were left completely deserted. Others might only have a handful of people. It was difficult for the survivors to plant and grow enough food to keep themselves alive.

The Lord of the Manor also had a problem. Unless he could persuade the peasants to work for him, he would not be able to grow any crops in his own fields. But if the peasants worked for him, they might starve because they had not done their own work. It was difficult to make the peasants work for the lord; they hid or ran away.

LORD 1

Some lords moved all their peasants into one village. Then at least they had one group of villagers who could grow enough food and do enough work. The land they abandoned was gradually overgrown and became forest again.

LORD 2

Some lords tried to keep all their land under cultivation by paying the peasants a wage. The peasants would be happy to work for their lord if they were not losing out, but still gaining something.

LORD 3

Some lords changed the type of farming to farming sheep. One peasant could look after a huge flock of sheep, but it took many people to grow crops on the same land. (Look at the section on wool.)

LORD 4

Some lords tried to carry on as before. They employed soldiers to force the peasants to work on their land, and bailiffs or stewards to collect the rent. This led to a lot of resentment. (Look at the section on the Peasants Revolt.)

- Complete the table for methods used by lords of the manor to keep the peasants working for them.
- Which do you think would be the most effective method? Why?

One step further .....

- How did the changes to society brought about by the Black Death alter the Feudal System?
- How was the king's attitude to his nobles and their service going to have to change?
- If you were a lord of the manor, how would you try to persuade people to work for you?
- Design a poster to show your ideas.

LORD	SOLUTION	DISADVANTAGES

This page may be photocopied for classroom use only

Many peasants found life in the country too hard after the Black Death. For some, the answer lay in escaping from their village to find a new life elsewhere.

Peasants belonged to their lord, so to run away was a crime. People who were married and had families would stay where they were, but young men in particular would want to find something better.

Some men would go to another village, usually where the lord of the manor paid a wage to people who worked his land. There were many court cases in medieval times when a lord claimed that a neighbour was stealing his workforce with a promise of high wages. Parliament tried to stop this happening by regulating the amount a peasant could be paid. This didn't work, and the result was inflation, caused by higher and higher wages.

Some men went to live in the forest. As they had no lord, they were outside the law, or OUTLAWS. Groups of outlaws lived together, usually by stealing and hunting for food. Both of these were illegal, and outlaws who were caught could expect no mercy from the courts. Unlike Robin Hood, their victims were usually poor peasants, who were an easy target.

The most popular place to go and hide was a town. Towns with charters had no lord, and they were full of people, so a stranger would not be noticed. If a man could prove to the town or borough council that he had lived in a town for a year and a day, and that he was not a beggar, he could become a FREEMAN. This meant that even if his lord found out where he was, he could not be forced to go back to his village.

The other way of escape was for a boy to be taken into a monastery to train as a monk. This needed the consent of his lord, but the lord was not likely to want to offend the church by refusing. Boys who had trained as clerics could work as clerks, friars or priests, as well as monks. One estimate is that by 1500, about a sixth of all the people in England were employed by the church.

- Make a list of the advantages and disadvantages of each way of escape from village life.
- Why was it difficult for a girl to leave the village?
- How were families tied to the village?

One step further .....

- What would be the effect on village life if many of the young men left?
- How could the lord combat the effect of the young men leaving, or persuade them to stay?
- What way of escape would suit different people? What would families be most likely to want for their sons?

Richard II became king in 1377. He was only ten. The country was ruled by his uncle, John of Gaunt, and other advisors.....

The peasants had been very badly treated. Many peasants had died in the Black Death. Yet the lords still wanted their work done. Some peasants got a wage for their work, but most did not, which was unfair. As there were fewer people to produce food and other goods, there was inflation and prices of everything went up.

There was also a war going on; the Hundred Years War against France. The king's uncle was in charge of this war, and taxes got higher and more frequent to pay for it. Finally, in 1381, a POLL TAX was introduced. All people over fifteen had to pay twelve pence. This was very unfair. In earlier taxes the peasants had only paid four pence, but rich men like the king's uncle had paid the equivalent of 1600 pence.

All over the country peasants could not pay the tax because it was too high. The king's soldiers took their animals, cooking pots and stores of food instead.

John Ball, a wandering priest, organised a protest. He said:
'When Adam delved and Eve span,
Who was then the gentleman?'
The angry peasants from Kent and Essex decided that the king did not understand what was happening. So they decided to go to London to tell him why they could not pay. On the way they killed lawyers and officials, and burnt official records.

● What does the word 'Poll' actually mean?
● What did the Poll Tax take no account of?
● How did it affect the peasants when the soldiers took their cooking pots and food stores?

One step further .....

● Work out what John Ball's rhyme meant. Who are the 'gentlemen'?
● Why did the peasants decide that the king did not know what was going on?
● What was the point in killing officials and burning records?
● What do you think the punishment was for rebellion? Does this help to explain how desperate the peasants were?

When the rebels reached London they made a man called Wat Tyler, who came from Kent, their general. The Londoners opened the gates of the city to the rebels. They went to the Tower of London and destroyed all of the official records they could find there. Some more officials were killed, including the Archbishop of Canterbury and the Lord Treasurer, who were both blamed for the tax.

The Lord Mayor of London was a brave man, but saw that he would be unable to get the rebels to leave until they had met the king. So he arranged a meeting between the king and rebels outside the city walls at Mile End, and then again at Smithfield.

Richard promised that he would tell lawyers to look at the tax, but Tyler said this was not enough. There was a scuffle as Tyler tried to get closer to the king, and the Lord Mayor drew his sword and killed Tyler.

The peasants were angry about the death of their leader, and moved towards the king. But Richard bravely shouted that he would be their new leader. To get the peasants to go home he promised he would meet all their demands, and he gave each man a charter (promise written on paper) to take away as proof.

As soon as the rebels had gone home Richard sent soldiers after them. Those who showed their charters only proved that they had been rebels, and were hanged! So most destroyed their charters.

Although the revolt did not work, it showed the lords that the peasants would rebel if their lives got too harsh. When they united they were a powerful force. So the landowners gradually began to change, although it took many years for the feudal system to die out.

- Why were the Londoners on the side of the rebels?
- Why was the Archbishop of Canterbury killed, when he was a churchman?
- Why did the Lord Mayor of London arrange the meetings outside the city walls?

One step further .....

- Richard was only fourteen at the time. How would you describe his actions during the revolt?
- What were the reasons for giving the rebels charters?
- Why were landowners forced to change as a result of the revolt? What might happen to them if they didn't?

The Arts in medieval times.....

STATUE OF ST GEORGE 1416

Ordinary people did not have the spare time or money to spend much on their own homes. It is hard for us to know how much decoration there was because most peasants' houses were made of materials that have rotted away.

Pictures and decoration are mainly found in churches, and the homes of rich noblemen. The churches were beautified to glorify God, and later on the rich copied some of these ideas.

The most easy form of decoration came in wall paintings. Travelling artists would paint pictures with religious themes on the wall of the church to help the people think about God as they were worshipping.

Later ideas included putting coloured, or stained, glass in the windows as glass pictures. Carvings of saints and occasionally small paintings on wood were also much prized.

Noblemen, and perhaps some peasants, copied the idea of painting decoration on the walls of their houses. A later idea was to weave or embroider a wall hanging to put on the wall. As well as providing colour, a tapestry hanging cut out draughts and made the house warmer. Glass might also be put in a few windows.

By the end of the medieval period there were more people with spare money to use on beautifying their homes, but the decoration still tended to be practical and permanent, rather than a movable form of art like ornaments or pictures.

● Why do we not know very much about how ordinary people decorated their homes?
● Not many wall paintings have survived. Can you think of reasons why they have disappeared?
● What do we have today to decorate the walls and windows of our homes?

One step further .....

● The style of church building gradually changed from 1066 to 1500. Try to find out the three basic styles that were used.
● Why didn't this affect how ordinary people built their homes?
● Why did it affect the way rich men built their castles or homes?
● Who would probably decide to build a new church? How did this affect the design?
● Who did most of the skilled church building?

Knowledge and Understanding of History. The development of the English Language.....

Very few people could read and write in medieval England. The Saxons had enjoyed hearing stories, but the Norman invaders spoke French or Latin, and did not understand these.

At a time when there was no indoor lighting except candles, and nearly everybody worked hard at physical work all day, the evenings were an important time of relaxation. People talked or sang or told stories. Story-tellers travelled around the country from house to house. But a book meant the story could be heard again and again.

Most early enjoyment of literature was simply a book being read aloud by a priest or monk. As only clerics could read and write, it is not surprising that the theme was usually religious. Most books were in French or Latin, which fewer and fewer English people spoke as their main language. But in the fourteenth century a French fashion grew up to read books about knights and love. The stories of King Arthur became popular.

By Edward III's reign English was the official language of the court and parliament. Geoffrey Chaucer wrote the first well-known book in English at this time. *The Canterbury Tales* was about a group of pilgrims travelling to Thomas Becket's shrine, and the stories they tell to pass the time on their journey. Chaucer's book was very popular, and led to a growing fashion for books in English.

Although more and more books were written in English, it was not until the invention of printing in the late fifteenth century that books were available to all who could afford them. Until then books were handwritten and very expensive. William Caxton, who brought printing to England in 1476, printed mainly English books, and *The Canterbury Tales* was one of the first books he produced. The introduction of printing meant many more people got the opportunity to learn to read.

- The stories of King Arthur were around long before the Normans. Why did it take so long for them to be written down?
- Why did people all sit together in the evenings, even in the homes of rich men?
- What sort of person could borrow or buy a book?

One step further .....

- Geoffrey Chaucer was a Londoner. How did this affect the type of English he wrote?
- People in different parts of the country could often not understand each other. How did the introduction of books in English help to overcome this?
- Caxton printed *The Canterbury Tales* over 100 years after they were first written. What does this tell you about their popularity?

Medieval Monarchy and Barons.....

All the way through the fifteenth century there were wars in England. This is because two powerful families, the Dukes of York and Lancaster, thought they had the right to the throne. These wars did not last all of the time, but flared up when kings died or were incompetent.

The wars were known as the Wars of the Roses because each side had a rose as an emblem, white for York and red for Lancaster.
Henry IV 1399-1413 (L) *murdered his cousin, King Richard II, to become king.*
Henry V 1413-1422 (L) *died young.*
Henry VI 1422-1461 (L) *became king at only 9 months old. He was ill and a weak man for most of his reign, and was overthrown by Edward of York.*
Edward IV 1461-1483 (Y) *overthrew the Lancastrians. He was a strong but popular king, who died suddenly at only 42.*
Edward V 1483 (2 months) (Y) *became king at 13 years old. There were immediate plots to take the throne from him, and he disappeared mysteriously in 1483.*
Richard III 1483-1485 (Y) *was the brother of Edward IV and uncle of Edward V. Some people suspected Edward V had been murdered on his orders. He was killed at the Battle of Bosworth in 1485.*
Henry VII 1485-1509 (L) *had fought Richard at Bosworth. Some people suspected he had ordered the death of Edward V, so he married Edward's sister, Elizabeth, to unite the two families.*

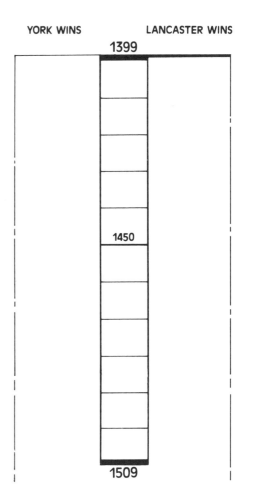

- Complete the diagram to show how the balance of power swung between the two sides in the Wars of the Roses.
- How would these wars affect the ordinary people?
- How did the system of inheriting the kingdom break down in the wars?

After the Battle of Bosworth England was at peace under the leadership of Henry's family, the Tudors, for the next 118 years. We use the date of the battle, 1485, as a turning point to mark the end of medieval times in this country.

One step further .....

- How did Henry Tudor try to unite the two sides?
- Why did people in medieval times dread having a young or incompetent king?
- How did the barons who fought on either side get their armies?
- How did the Wars of the Roses weaken the feudal system so much that it had collapsed by 1485?

the Battle of Bosworth.....2

History cannot really be divided up into 'chunks of time'. But the Battle of Bosworth in 1485 is a convenient date, as the ideas of the Middle Ages were already slowly dying out throughout the country, and newer ideas were replacing the ideas of the Normans.

The feudal system was dying out. Many tenants now paid money as taxes to the king instead of owing him service as a knight.

Peasants were more likely to own their own land and to get paid when they worked for their lord. In return they paid rent. They no longer belonged to the land.

Farming concentrated on sheep and wool production instead of grain. This was making England a rich country.

More and more people lived in towns and cities. People were more interested in art and literature.

The barons had destroyed themselves through fighting each other in the Wars of the Roses. Henry VII kept strict controls on the power of the nobles.

Wales now belonged to England, and Scotland and England lived as neighbours. But England had lost all of her continental possessions except the town of Calais.

● What do you think was the most important change that had taken place during the Middle Ages?

But some things had not changed.

The church remained powerful, and in control of about a quarter of the land and employing a sixth of the population.

Science and medicine had not changed. People still did not know what caused disease, and treated it through herbal medicine.

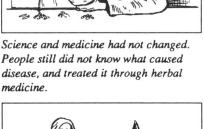

Women still had no rights and belonged to their husbands or fathers.

The monasteries still looked after education, hospitals and welfare.

Ordinary people still had no say at all in the way the country was governed.

One step further .....

● Imagine you are living in London in 1500. Write a letter describing how your life is different to the type of life you would have led 400 years ago.

glossary

APPRENTICE	a boy learning a craft over a fixed time
ARCHER	a person who shoots with a bow and arrows
BLACK DEATH	a form of plague
CANON	to do with the church, church law
CAUTERISE	to burn away for medical reasons
CHARTER	a list of the rights of people or towns
CHASTITY	to not have a sexual relationship
CLERGY	a person who was an official of the church
CRUSADE	a Christian holy war
CURFEW	a time of day when people were meant to stay indoors
FEUDAL SYSTEM	a form of government when land is held in return for service
FREEMAN	a person who does not have to obey a lord
FRIAR	a monk who lives in the community
GOODWIFE	a local woman with medical skills
GUERILLA	a member of a small group of fighters, not an army
GUILD	a society of craftsmen who look after standards of work and the welfare of guild members
HEAVEN	the place where God lives, where the good go
HELL	the place where the Devil lives, where the bad go
INTERDICT	a ban on church services
JOURNEYMAN	a craftsman who works for a master craftsman
JUDGEMENT DAY	the end of the world, when God decides who goes to Heaven and Hell
KNIGHT	a soldier on horseback (Norman title)
LATIN	the language of the church and the educated
LORD	a title given to the person who ruled peasants
MARCHES	the border area between England and Wales
MASTERPIECE	the best work of an apprentice
MERCHANT	a person who bought and sold goods
MONARCH	government by a king
MONASTERY	a separate community where men or women lived religious lives
OBEDIENCE	doing what one is told without arguing
ORDER	type of religious group
OUTLAW	a person who has escaped from his lord
PARLIAMENT	a group of men chosen to advise the king
POLL TAX	a tax everyone has to pay equally
POVERTY	not having enough necessities of life
REVOLT	to fight against
TENANT	a person whose property is held in return for payment
TITHE	a tenth of earnings tax to the church
WATTLE AND DAUB	woven frame of twigs and mud